PRAISE FOR MIGHTIER–

MW00526726

"In challenging times like these, poetry and t.. .... g... .... lective experience, enrich our understanding with new insight and perspective, challenge us and inspire us. CAPS anthologies achieve this consistently by bringing together gifted artists from the Hudson Valley and across the world, and we thank you for the opportunity to explore perspectives on social justice, injustice, and liberation through this vibrant collection of work."

— *Senator Jen Metzger*
New York State Senate, 42nd District

"To inspire change, we must not shy away from difficult conversations and perhaps now more than ever, poetry provides an outlet to communicate with one other in a unique and beautiful way about important issues. Poet Gold's passion and energy for poetry is evident in all she does; she shared that passion throughout the county for two years as our Dutchess County Poet Laureate, and again as curator of this meaningful anthology."

— *Marc Molinaro*
Dutchess County Executive

"As we face a pandemic not unprecedented, as our nation is being fueled by hate trying for a TBT1619...open, honest, and vulnerable conversations while listening with our hearts and not our egos—these are all important factors in shifting that whole trajectory. Harambee (Kingston, NY) celebrates this assemblage of celebrated poets, writers, and slam artists of all nations, backgrounds, and colours as we call upon our ancestors to help us continue the dialogue, with all mutual respect, on how we will stand our ground as a coming together of people...with one heart, one love...by all and every means necessary."

— *Tyrone Wilson*
Founder, Harambee Kingston NY
Ulster County Commissioner of Human Resources

"Artists—the poets, writers, painters, performers, muralists, and musicians—have the ability to distill the world they live in through their art. They are today's prophets, philosophers, and truth tellers that make sense of our lives and societies.
This anthology put together in 2020 captures the urgent voices of poets harmonizing with the voices of the oppressed, the forgotten, the newly awakened, and the ignored. The call for change is clear, but as John Lewis stated, sometimes we need to get into necessary trouble to make change.
These poems speak of memories, outrage, and a call for change using voices built through resiliency, yet moving ahead with hope."

— *Linda Marston-Reid*
visual artist, art writer
Executive Director, Arts Mid-Hudson, NY

"In the two decades in which I've been a CAPS fan, I have been wowed time and again by the poets and the poetry of my beloved Hudson Valley. What you hold in your hands is but the tip of a glorious iceberg, but what a refreshing tip it is!"

— *John Leonard Pielmeier,* actor, poet,
playwright *(Agnes of God, The Boys of Winter, Hook's Tale, The Exorcist)*
novelist, *(Hook's Tale)*; screenwriter *(The Pillars of The Earth)*

"This anthology captures the vital community of writers living in the Hudson Valley. Calling All Poets over the course of twenty years as evidenced in this volume has nurtured and supported numerous poets, with distinct voices, approaches, styles, and genres. This is a rich and compelling collection of works that speaks deeply to many aspects of the human experience and provides illumination; childhood memories, family relationships, lost love, the search for the meaning in existence, and the witnessing of injustice are all powerfully portrayed. I appreciate the range of form and style from lyric poems to personal and prose poetry , from rich descriptive sensory pieces to philosophical inquiries and surreal and mythic visions. This is a volume that deserves to be read many times, and each time a reader will find new poetic treasures."

— *Jan Zlotnik Schmidt,* SUNY Distinguished Teaching Professor
co-editor of *A Slant of Light: Contemporary Women Writers of the Hudson Valley*

"Calling All Poets has successfully created a diverse community of poets and writers who support one another. Whenever I'm there, I feel as if I am part of something bigger, a movement in the arts. In addition, they have embraced technology, streaming readers outside the area live and broadcasting the events online. Calling all Poets is the best series in the Hudson Valley!

— *Rebecca Schumejda,* poet
Cadillac Men, Waiting at the Dead End Diner

"CAPS is about poetry of course. But it's also about community, how it's actually created a community of diverse personalities and backgrounds that come together each month to speak in the one language we all know: The spoken word. Every month there's a mark on the calendar that we all look forward to."

— *Ken Holland,* poet, Pushcart nominee

"The Hudson Valley boasts a plethora of fascinating poets whose active participation in readings and local events makes them a reliable source of wisdom and inspiration."

— *Dr. Lucia Cherciu,* poet
Lepădarea de Limbă *(The Abandonment of Language)*

"The Hudson Valley gives voice to writers and poets who have something of value to say and a comfortable environment for accomplishing this important endeavor. From the caves of Rosendale to the richness of Roost Studios, the Hudson Valley has nurtured me and advanced my career."

— *Eddie Bell*, author, poet
Capt's Dreaming Chair, Festival of Tears

"The Hudson Valley is one of the most vibrant and exciting poetry regions in the country and Calling All Poets at in Beacon is a centerpiece for the power of words. I feel fortunate to be part of this creative current and to be able to share the art of language with the hundreds of writers I've met and whose works I've been able to read and hear over the years."

— *Laurence Carr*, author
Pancake Hollow Primer; editor: *Reflecting Pool: Poets and the Creative Process* and *Riverine*; co-editor of *WaterWrites* and *A Slant of Light* (Codhill Press)

"Thanks to both the many hardworking poetry hosts and the scores of poets who come out to share their work it sometimes seems one could attend a reading every day. And the truly wonderful thing is that the region is home to a number of extremely gifted poets who can leave an audience wishing their reading would never end."

— *Matthew J. Spireng*, poet, and three time Pushcart nominee

"I can't imagine living anywhere else in the world. Where else could I find the variety, the devotion, the matter-of-fact respect for poetry not just as an art but a fact of life? From the poetry gangs of Albany to the lost souls of Orange County, I believe the Hudson Valley provides a unique climate for poets of all inclinations to share their work in a supportive environment, a gift not always available to other creators."

— *Cheryl A. Rice*, poet
My Minnesota Boyhood, Moses Parts The Tulips

"Generations of painters have drawn inspiration from the age-worn corrugations in Hudson Valley landscapes and the glow of the skies overhead after late-summer thunderstorms give way to dusk. Folk singers impassioned by the rainbow taint of pollutants in the fabled Hudson River gave voice to the modern environmental movement. This latest collection of verse penned by the region's poets—from acidic to comedic to political to pastoral—shows how fertile the ground here is for the written and spoken word, as well. Dive in!"

— *Andy Revkin*, longtime environmental journalist, sometime songwriter

"The CAPS Anthology is living proof that poetry, literature and those who continue to create and/or appreciate it are not defined by their location, education, pigmentation or social station. In 2019, The Anthology's home base, the historic Hudson Valley, retains the same magical spirit that inspired 19th Century visual artists to excel and reflect their surroundings. After reading this new collection in the latest CAPS Anthology, we all look forward to MORE!!! Thank you Calling All Poets and all of today's poets for inspiring us and our kids by sharing words and images of lasting value!!"

— *David Amram*, conductor, composer
with Jack Kerouac, the undisputed co-founder of what has become *Jazzoetry*

"The twentieth anniversary Calling All Poets Anthology consists of some of the best poems by more than forty poets included in the CAPS poetry reading series. The collection is dedicated to Donald Lev (1936-2018) who edited and published Home Planet News, among countless contributions to the literary community. Among the mellifluous vein of talented poets, a sample includes Laurence Carr, Donald Lev, Susan Hoover, Mary Makofske, Roger Aplon, Irene O'Garden, Rebecca Schumejda, Matthew J. Spireng, Lucia Cherciu, Ruth Danon, Bertha Rogers, Jim Eve, Pauline Uchmanowicz, and Mike Jurkovic. This is an anthology that speaks to the current political climate, to nature and climate change, to family dynamics and all phases of human life. Whether shouts or celebrations, prayers or meditations, these poems demonstrate that the Hudson River a shelter for poets and dreamers today just as it once was for Hudson River School painters in the nineteenth century.

— *Margo Taft Stever*, author
Cracked Piano (CavanKerry Press, 2019)

"What if the poets of the Hudson Valley had a party and everybody came? This hospitable and yet lively (read: rockin') anthology catches that spirit. This isn't a Hudson River School of poetry. It's a Hudson Valley lyric line dance. Everyone's invited. Come on down."

— *TR Hummer*, poet
Eon (LSU Press, 2018), After The Afterlife (Acre Books, 2018),
The Infinity Sessions (Southern Messenger Poets, 2005)

"The varied crowd Calling All Poets attracts makes for lively nights. It's rare that we have a dull evening. The fact that the hosts are welcoming and gracious for the presence of a supportive crowd speaks volumes. You don't have nearly the sense of camaraderie anywhere else."

— *Christopher Wheeling*, poet, CAPS photographer

"I believe that if CAPS continues on the path it is now blazing it will become an important milestone in the growth of American Poetry."

— *Glenn Werner*, poet
Premeditated Contrition and other poems, CAPS Tech Czar

"Poets have grown up at CAPS."

— *Jim Eve*, poet, founder, co-host, Calling All Poets

Mightier

Poets For Social Justice

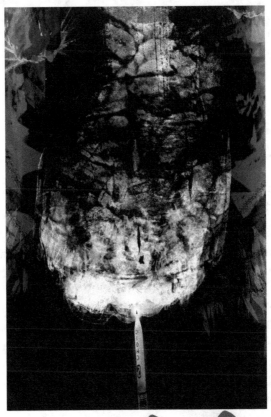

mightier

POETS FOR SOCIAL JUSTICE

EDITED BY POET GOLD

CAPS
PRESS

CAPS, CAPS Press, and its logos are copyrights © 2020 of Calling All Poets, Inc
Calling All Poets, Inc (CAPS)
79 Sargent Ave Beacon NY 12508

callingallpoets.net

Ordering Information:
For details, contact info@callingallpoets.net.

Print ISBN: 978-0-9973258-4-3
eBook ISBN: 978-0-9973258-5-0

Printed in the United States of America

First Edition

Design, production, editing, and illustration credits:

Book design and production: small packages, inc
smallpackages.com

Cover Image: Greg Correll
gregcorrell.com

Editor: Poet Gold
instagram.com/_poetgold_/
linkedin.com/in/poetgoldbgw/

"At the moment when I was on the bridge
and began to fall, I really thought it was
my last protest, my last march.
I thought I saw death and I thought
'it's okay, it's all right—
I am doing what I am supposed to do.'"

— *John Lewis, 1940-2020*

CONTENTS

The Poems

Bios

Poets are people too.
We rise in protest.
We face the injustice.

We reach for the soul.

In the dauntless words that follow, the poets gather w/their children, their peers, their elders at the barricades. Armed w/answers. Armed w/prayers. But not with absolution. No, forgiveness comes from doing right.

Stand up. Stay healthy. Stay strong.

mike jurkovic

aug 20

The poetic voice...

Amidst Covid-19, racial unrest, political mayhem, the poet's voice becomes vital in removing the noise to hear the song. In unjust times, most poets will invoke their artivism through words of hope, despair, revolt, rage, laughter conveying the people's voice. When I came across the email request to act as editor for *Mightier – Poets for Social Justice*, I responded affirmatively.

With projects such as this one, you never know what you will receive from your fellow poets. You only hope the submissions will meet the ask. I was pleasantly surprised the poems submitted did. My role in the process became to align the poetic styles and voices in a way that is fluid for the reader whether they were a poet or not, without sacrificing the individual persona contained in each poem. There were a few subtle style edits, but nothing major.

We are living in a time of fragility, where some will break, but most will survive. I believe we are strong. For the poems contained within speak to our strength, our love, our resilience, our ugly truth in America, and the beauty of the idea of an America. Without sounding trite, if the sun rises, we can potentially change any circumstance we may find ourselves in. Never lose hope but be ready to stand up for what you know is right in your soul.

Poet Gold

Editor

BE THE
POEM

No doubt I have a bias
I am going to ask of you to be poetry
to be the poem in your life
to be that which moves you
stirs you like a lover's first kiss
compelling you to believe
you are now super human
pumping with adrenaline
capable of conquering anything
WOW

Be the poem
imagine sunsets with orange hues
    across the sky
as the stars ascend to blanket the night
when things go dark, be the light
    in your life
Be the poem

Be the poem
that teaches, reaches
circles the universe
through quatrains, sonnets
prose and free verse
let it be Mozart to a hip hop beat
ballet performed on black top and concrete
let it be imaginative, soulful,
    eloquently stated
and unique
Be the poem

Be the poem
that chooses to be fearless
never imprisons the heart
beckons the soul to rain tears
when you're falling apart
Be the poem

Be the poem
that heals and learns to forgive
releasing thunderous anger and hate
so, you may truly live
and if there comes a day
you should fall ill
know that cure
may not come in the form of a pill
but in the lines of poetry
that will be more than a prayer
it will shout hallelujah
your salvation will be there
Be the poem

Be the poem
that breathes the breath
to dream out loud
discover the wonder
residing above the clouds
for Helios chariot
brings hope with each day
the time is now
to make life your way
board your ship
set sail to sea
be brave
be the poem in your life
may your life be poetry.

—*Poet Gold*
September 20

The Poems

JUNETEENTH

Kate Hymes

The people of Texas are informed
                all slaves are free
                    absolute equality
    of personal rights
    and rights of property
The freedmen
    remain quietly
at their present homes and work
    for wages
            will not be allowed to collect
will not be supported in idleness

Note:

> [Official.]
> HEADQUARTERS DISTRICT OF TEXAS. }
> GALVESTON TEXAS, June 19, 1865. }
> *General Orders, No. 3.*
>   The people are informed that, in accordance with
> a proclamation from the Executive of the United
> States, all slaves are free. This involves an abso-
> lute equality of personal rights and rights of prop-
> erty, between former masters and slaves, and the
> connection heretofore existing between them, be-
> comes that between employer and hired labor.—
> The Freedmen are advised to remain at their pres-
> ent homes, and work for wages. They are inform-
> ed that they will not be allowed to collect at mili-
> tary posts; and that they will not be supported in
> idleness either there or elsewhere.   By order of
>   Major-General GRANGER.
> (Signed,)   F. W. EMERY, Maj. & A. A. G.

What Do White Folks Know Of Racism In America?

Roger Aplon

They either know they don't know or they're, once more, deceiving themselves.
What culture is free from intolerance,
Lacks a line-in-the-sand that cannot be crossed for fear of arrest or even death?
No? Not here? Not in these U S of A?
You who would deny
Are deaf & blind to our history.
We have lived a national lie since our formation
When our founders declared "... all men are created equal"
But not our slaves.
Demand
"Enough of this hypocrisy"
Confront our duplicity
& rip the blindfold
From the face
Of justice.

Love vs Hate

Regi Wroteit

Listen. Observe. Validate. Empathize.
Living in a world where people would rather
Humiliate. Agitate. Trigger. Eliminate…
Is so exhausting. Still, love and light will shine.
I have the courage to survive.
Do you?

No More

Regi Wroteit

No one asked you to bestow your hate towards me,
Overtly or covered up.

My plea for mankind, even though they are
Obsessed with skin color, is to
Reevaluate your logic, accept the diversity all around
Enlighten the self with love's definition, agape for all.

Reassess the threat I supposedly hold towards you when
Actually I'm trying to just live and survive this game of life with you
Calling onto others with nothing but respect,
Initiating genuine agape love and care
Stop attacking innocent humans for just being alive.
Meet me in the garden of peace where there will be

N.O. M.O.R.E. R.A.C.I.S.M.

closer now

Greg Correll

From a distance we are bugs,
dots of color underfoot, scrabbling
over the thin skin we call home.

Kissing and killing, holding grudges,
planning meals, reading and writing—
up-and-at-em? down-in the-dumps?
all looks the same, from up here.

up dress eat work eat sit undress down
        —we disappear into wheeled machines,
                reappear when they spit us out
        —so busy, so frantic, so earnest
up dress eat work eat sit undress down
          —over and over and over until we fall over.

See us as performers: endless displays of affection
         and hilarity, of grief and rage and boredom.
So easily distracted, so hard to wake up.

Watch us: we pulse. Every aspect trembles—
         we flare out as grief twists, bend in as love binds.
From a distance these are pointless transformations.

Can you see us? We all have two legs.
We wave our arms around.
Sooner or later we pair off.
It all seems repetitive and random.

See our essential mistake? *Some are denied.*
Some are stepped on, burned up, kept in jars.
Some are toyed with, raged upon, dragged under.
Some are ignored to death.

Every collective error magnifies pain,
        every collective pretense dulls over time.
We are the same, the way we insist on differences,
        and take each other for granted.

Closer now. Close enough to see and be seen—
        to step in when a child is struck,
        to step up when someone's dignity is taken.

The awkward place of disruption and discovery.
Close enough to see kin, not vermin, to recognize
        injustice for what it is: fearful greed.
Close enough to never be denied.
Close enough that when hatred extinguishes the light,
        we are ready with a fistful of matches.

The Worst Politicians

Chris Collins

sterile impotent these
politicians shout out
in prime time

their wives
lovingly loyal
cling to their vine

not from affection
but to preserve
their goldmine

the curtain that
veils a man's dark deeds
while he bloviates in prime

time for the masses
to keep them massed
most of the time

their secret pleasures
in a world they control
costs them their spine

ego id-driven impulsive
glued to power with
superego long in decline

discourage the endless
masses that depend
on every dime

then there's the rest —
the oppressed — just waiting
and biding their time

Killer-Men

Chris Collins

killer-men are out there having fun
some are teens with military guns
bullet-holing people with their venom
wreaking havoc with their killer-weapons

histories of domestic violence
predation's part of their experience
they are cult-like conditioned actors
with role models and benefactors

victims themselves of their culture's ills
they force people behind window sills
with hateful rhetoric they help create
grief for others that does not dare abate

thoughts and prayers are constant offerings
and despite all of the peoples' sufferings
the hate pervades many people's lives
it's time to destroy it - time to rise

We Are Not Going Back

Cassandra Clarke

We battle a strange helplessness
But behind the resilience is a stranger faith
Society has blocked us and was hiding our truths, burning us physically
        and mentally too, but we still rise and put on our boots
Emerging from the ambers and soot are Black and Brown lives
        you cannot silence

At the moment of the kill, our hearts laid still
We could not turn away, our eyes had to stay to witness again,
        that familiar hate and kill
Knowing you could not take him down, without a gun
        and could not catch him if you had to run,
Anger
Anger that he had courage to be in security work
Anger that he supported his daughter
Anger that he could have a Black man's legacy

So you came in for the kill, repositioned your knee,
        till Floyd was dead and still
You had to figure out how to explain a DAR, or
        did something happen at the bar?
Did Floyd say he would buy a new car?
Had Racism brought you that far?
Your hate could not have Floyd, riding around like a star
Imagine that was supposed to be a
"beat down," as if thoughts could be pressed from Floyd's mind,
        wearing your uniform of anti-crime

Now his memory is in all corners of the world

It has contributed to our ability to ride on even higher ground! Though
having been horribly racially bound, resulting in our walking around
so twisted that our entire being is often in the shape of a frown

I will keep my frown because we are not going back

Image: Cassandra Clarke

When No Good Word

Stephanie Laterza

So much of motherhood is surviving the night, an emergency waiting
room crowded with inadvertent burns, sudden poisonings, falls,
the fault of unfathomable seconds. The scorch of tears, adrenaline

burning a mother's eyes awake, her heart caught, pulsing
in her throat, ribs battered with the sound, waiting, pleading, until some
good word arrives, her child is breathing.
They can go home.

What then when no good
word arrives for a mother. Her son can't breathe.
He can't go home.

Another son cried out to his mother
as a cop crushed his lungs in the street,
kneeling on his neck for 8 minutes and 46 seconds.
In war, dying soldiers always cry out
for their mothers.

What then when no good
word arrives for a mother. The cops shot her daughter. Eight times.
While she slept in her home. After her sleepless shifts as a paramedic
reviving people during the pandemic. No medics tried to revive her.
What then when no good
word arrives for a mother. Two men shot her son.
They'd chased him in a truck while he jogged in the afternoon.
He's never coming home.

What then when no good
word arrives for a mother. A vigilante shot her son for walking
down a street where he was visiting family.
He's not coming home.

What then when no good
word arrives for a mother. The cops shot her son dead in his car
in front of his girlfriend in the front seat, and her four-year-old daughter
in the backseat.
Afterwards, her daughter cradled her own mother, pleading and crying
that she didn't want her to die too.

Word arrives, too, for the school children whom her son helped
when they couldn't pay their lunch debt,
whose allergies he knew, who needed, who waited for him too
to come home.

What then when no good
word reaches a mother, two men shot her son
down South where he was visiting family.
A white woman said he groped her, a lie
like so many.
After kidnapping, then torturing him overnight in a shed,
where passing witnesses heard him cry out for his mother,
they shot him in the head, then threw his body in a river.

There could never be a metaphor as clear as those photos.

What then when no good
word arrives for a mother again and then
again, then again what then
will you do then, and again,
until no more no good
word arrives for a mother.

Image: Lucy

Miles Back

Mike Jurkovic

I brushed up on my physics miles back.
So there's no conning me This two for one
in the waiting room Waiting for hellhounds
to catch our scent, Our odor of sin,
the miles few between us.

I don't care what the plan-o-gram says.
I'm holding the line right here
in contempt of the nightshift's opposition.
Someone's gotta or we're all fighting each other
despite what we know.
The plan-o-gram. The plan-o-gram
God fuck their plan-o-gram
that keeps us seething.

This is their game: Me killing you
for a color, a carrot, a god.
From hovels we roam hand to hand, door to door
An army vengeful, powered by holy fuel.

Everything's a target but shouldn't be.
Trump should be.
And all the foaming dogs like him.

But enough of this when
I'm trying to talk peace.
For what win is a war
that leaves children crying?
Women w/child in tears?
City and town, shrapnel and flak?
Our good books morbid slogans?
It's no war at all, of course
it's defeat. Pure and simple,
A rout. Their flag above it all.

The Up-slide

Amanda Russell

There I stood in the summer beneath a ginkgo tree.
A white mother at a park on G Street
with my two-year-old son. We were in our neighborhood:
the part of town that's not quite the center but full of
brick streets, old frame houses sliced into apartments and 16-plexes;
the part of town where we are all renters sharing sidewalks and parks.
Standing just a few feet from us was a Black father playing with his son.

I noticed the boy was climbing up the slide, and the father
wasn't telling him the usual phrases like, "what are you doing"
or "get down from there" or "take the stairs."
He was telling him, "You never, ever, give up. Keep going."

Even then I thought this man wasn't just teaching his son
to climb slides. Maybe he was equipping him for life— teaching
him hope bests gravity and determination stomps strife.

The boy kept climbing, but his blue sandals started to slip.
His father leaned in whispering, "You never give up. Keep going."
And just then it began to rain.

Most everyone was ending their game and giving waves,
but the boy was still climbing the up-slide.
We turned to leave. Holding hands, my son and I headed
for the street. And that's when I turned back to see:
He made it to the top with his father cheering him on.
Then he turned right around to slide back down,
giggling all the way into his father's waiting arms.

Dear Lady Liberty

Amanda Russell

> *"Give me your tired, your poor,*
> *Your huddled masses yearning to breathe free,*
> *The wretched refuse of your teeming shore.*
> *Send these, the homeless, tempest-tost to me,*
> *I lift my lamp beside the golden door."*
>   -from *"The New Colossus"* by Emma Lazarus

You stand in New York Harbor. Exalted. America's Madonna
holding not a Child but a torch with a gilded flame. Your gaze
fixed out to sea, welcoming immigrants to the land of opportunity.

Lady Liberty, I need to know: from the height at which you stand,
do you see the tempest swelling up in your own land:
the injustice, the hunger, the ignorance, the murders,
the equality crippled by crooked infrastructures?

Could you turn your gaze to the melting pot
at boiling point: the children of immigrants,
slaves and indigenous peoples- the generations
already American? Do you see the tired, the poor,
the huddled masses still yearning to breathe free?

Are you a beacon of hope or warning?
Have your mild eyes witnessed the struggle and sweat
of not yet, the horrors of America's promise unkept?
Could you turn around to face the mainland
and extend your invitation to the oppressed
voices within your teeming shores?
Mother of Exiles, could you lower your lamp
and light this side of our golden door?

After the Election Oakland Burns Down

Sandra Yannone

Tonight I woke and wept for liberation
and for a different ghost ship than usual,
one not sunk this time by ice and greed,
but extinguished by smoke and neglect.
I switched on my bedside lamp
to keep at bay the lack of light
which is different than discouraging
the power of the dark. The dark provokes
dreams. The dark fertilizes ground.
The dark is my hand combing through
my hair's unstarried night.

A vote is not a siren, not a fire
engine screaming to a find a blaze
in progress. A vote is a hand
extended after smolder, after too much
hate, after candidate(s) said too little,
too much, too late, conflagrates.
I didn't vote to slap anyone
in the face. I didn't vote
to silence a people.
To silence anyone,
cuts off the power
to the lights, which, I repeat, is
not the same as the necessity
to enrich the dark.

Never shut this window to even a senseless night.
Stay open to the hands that reach out,
look out, for you like the forest ranger
who lives alone for months in the watchtower,
searching out the infant fires before the juniper trees
burn their old growth down.

Occupy Sonnet

Sandra Yannone

Because everything is broken in this
country of squandered and pillaged
dreams, even the sonnet's usual bliss
can't right itself in fourteen jagged

lines. When all is said and done,
this sonnet will list like the Andrea
Doria, mortally wounded off the stone
coast of New England, her swaying

lifeboats, unhinged from their davits,
the syllables too far and few between
governments, banks, and poets
to save everyone from the preened,

sanctioned drowning. So this sonnet ends.

Phone Pole Poetry

Jean O'Neill

It all started last night
Talking in the grass
Something about restoring ones faith
In Humanity
How Does One Do That?
From within
From without
From talking in the grass

Phone Pole Poetry

Douglass Ridgeway

I rise in the morning foggy.
Failing. Trying to remember what we talked about last night.
So I start over. Try to clear my mind.
Think about my dying lawn not my faith nor humanity.
I spend time figuring out the sex of my pumpkin flowers not this crazy world.
Feeling the heat already - oppression.
Watching the birds makes me want more.
I'm not ready for this kind of connection.
There's responsibility in a response.
But silence is not an option.

THERE IS PERHAPS NO BETTER DEMONSRATION OF THE FOLLY OF HUMAN CONCEITS THAN THIS DISTANT IMAGE OF OUR TINY WORLD. TO ME, IT UNDERSCORES OUR RESPONSIBILITY TO DEAL MORE KINDLY WITH ONE ANOTHER, AND TO PRESERVE AND CHERISH THE PALE BLUE DOT, THE ONLY HOME WE'VE EVER KNOWN.

—CARL SAGAN, 1994

Image: Matt Maley

Dreams

Cheryl A. Rice

My body a muddle of joints succumbing to a soft routine,
spreads across the blooming consciousness of quarantine.
Time still has a shape, shadow defined by sunlight,
firecrackers, a few good souls out to break our solitude
with guest star visits in my dreams.
There is still a nine-to-five for me,
a rarity in these pandemic hours.
I perform my usual tasks- phone calls, input, spreadsheets
with no assurance that data will keep me employed.

My taste for crafts dulled, yarn in the basement
remains neatly skeined, needled projects hang threadless,
folded roughly and shoved behind the curtains,
alcove that in olden times held a Murphy bed,
times before me when a probable woodstove
gave all the heat and light a body could bear.

Whatever curve there was in me is flattening
faster than any mapped disease.
Don't look to me for answers, my Jurassic lover.
These times remind me of how little I control,
how much our daily bread depends on progress,
how soon the winds of wheat might scatter
all we have claimed as ours.

I seek the slumber tonight of the otherwise occupied,
consumed with afterlife comforts of my dearly departed,
kinder in death and dark than in their
days on earth.

Feejee

Cheryl A. Rice

The world is a lot smaller than I suspected.
Even after twelve hours in the Philly airport,
I knew the place from end to end like the back of my hand.
There is nowhere these days where our own modern plague hasn't reached—
Feejee, birthplace of the famous mermaid, merman tribe,
even has a few tired lungs to account for,
days of South Seas bliss on pause.

And the quarantine we read about in the novels of Dickens,
Victorian bedclothes hosting battles in the land of counterpane,
gentle Mother in her mobcap bringing beef tea and milk punch
is nothing like our daily restrictions—
most well, some working from home, our computers,
like our bodies, adapt readily to work or play.
Movies we stream on the brook of electric vaudeville
we invite each night onto our TV stages
become our only option, theatres shuttered,
homey Zoom sing-alongs standing in for ensemble productions.

And with the relative silence, school buses dead in their lot,
birds believe they've reclaimed the neighborhood,
chant their sensual litany louder, faster, over and over.
Ambulances, fire sirens seem more frequent,
but it's just unpolluted air carrying their
tragic notices without distraction.

I resent recording impressions of these days,
knowing how brisk competition will be—
fundraisers, anthologies.
I have my private vision of Earth as a ragged ball,
no ballast, falling from its ancient rotation,
gravity suddenly a factor, into the black so
oceans can't be sorted from shadows.
I feel the pain of a hundred years from now,
when these few months become a footnote,
when we remove our masks to reveal again
our naked selves, untrimmed, unclean,
ready for nothing.

Pain

Meghan Sullivan

Pain is more palatable than charcuterie board
More direct than DNR order
More friendly than latex neighbor
More staking than to forgive grandmothers

It is most sad and lonely
And lonely hates a crowd
A crown given out at a pity party
Is no crown for survivor

Pain is less a point finger
Less here nor there
Less brie or barrel-aged
Less night owl catches worm

It is most simple and human
And more it is not one of a kind
Than all the grapes mourners snack on are
Pitted in bloody mornings with no stoop nor paper

Take 'Em Down

Meghan Sullivan

A swell overcomes the French Quarter
Moment of silence as requested by speaker
More stifling than feels like 102 degree temperature

You know tourist tax dollars don't come to our city
Schools are breaking our babies backs
You know white educators lacking boundaries
Calling scholars babies is dangerous

Andrew Jackson as a central figure in Creole center is curious
And curriculums need cultural relevance beyond Katrina
Little boys need raise an eyebrow at white ladies in free hugs t-shirts

You know about Devonte, right?
You remember the Hart Tribe, right?
You're no Amy Cooper, right?

Poboys and black people
are not to be commodified, vilified, why
Ask questions when the answers have been screamed
Have turned rally cry
Have proceeded proclamations
like Say Her Name

Names that need to be taught to students
Names of activists
Human beings that are worth more than Lincoln's two cents
Or charter system CEO piggy banks

A breeze overcomes the French Quarter
Call to action as requested by speaker
More immediate than feels like 102 degree temperature

More Hephaestus Than Apollo

Stephanie JT Russell

I know you miss the eon before
they slashed your budget. When
production and demand ran free.
Plenty of time to wait out an idea,
watch its manifold petals lazily
coruscate like basalt brewing
in a drowsy old volcano.

But Apollo's languid ego festered:
barely behind your back, at one
of his millennium-long astral orgies,
murmuring, Olympia will be stripped
bare if we continue allotting luxuries
to lesser forms. Then lifting his perfect
septum—proof of the anointed sigil
to breed a race of fey, self-cherishing
geniuses, from whose company your
like was disjected in fevered haste.

Given no recourse by your embarrassed,
wine-shambled father—

> dreadfully sorry, boy, but you know mother
> adores her Australian Opal bidet, and uncle
> his autumn-sealskin slippers. And then
> there's the legion of half-blood little bastards
> whose breeders come banging at my gates,
> demanding demigod status or elaborate housing
> on Syphonos, and well, you know sacrifices
> are necessary to keep this thing in order—

you slouched into the toilet and split yourself
into a serviceable legion of labor.

A broken crucible teeters atop the forge,
reminding you that nothing stays whole
under incalescent brutality. On our midnight
visit, we are staggered by the sight of you
drawing back the furnace door, smiling
to expose the feral, condensed sun roaring
in its viscera. The platinum horses will
be transparent, you say. Of this much I
am certain.

Visitation

or: The Ancestors Finally Reject Our Childish Pleas for Clemency

Stephanie JT Russell

In the end, our failure to raise a visitation
became intolerable. With every grotto sealed—

      long abandoned in the milky tracks
      of goat-herding children and their minion
      trudging the bleached yellow hillside—

we rummaged the blurred, indolent shallows
at the furthest lip of the land. Face down in the muddle,
fingers snaking through confused bottom weeds,
we twisted a root and delivered it from the chill, defiant muck.
Then raised our heads to the cracking blow of a daylight
that refused to diminish its sum for our sake.

Fever-blind, we sped headlong to periphery,
haphazard shards of hope
whirling through our dazed, mute esophagus,
summoning the waters of earth
to the stinging white brine of our misbegotten thirst,
surging tiny pathetic waves abreast Gibraltar's atoms
as if that stony ecstasy of silent rock might erode
and bare its fugitive fossil,
which might dare speak
given that words might have bones,
sovereign locomotion, power of direction—

      headlong into blank astringent fact,
      the tincture we tasted by night—

where last we went together
mining ice for fossil memory,
and watched its rime burn away
beneath dawn-rise,
in whose heat we hid the weeping sun
revolving in our belly,
awaiting birth into a sky,
any sky—
any sky at all.

toy soldiers

Bruce Weber

my daddy bought me a thousand toy soldiers
and i play war whenever i'm alone.
sometimes in the early morning light
i arrange them in infantries
along the ridges and valleys of my bed sheets
sending hundreds to their death
in the cauldron of wrinkles and folds.
someday i'm going to shoot my enemies
that's what my daddy tells me.
now me and my buddies
go rat a tat tat
and somebody falls down
but they're only fooling.
anyway i prefer playing with my soldiers.
sometimes i fight the battle of gettysburg
over and over on my bed
arranging the blanket
like devil's den or cemetery ridge.
i get a lot of satisfaction
watching rebels fall.
this is more fun
than dancing with all those silly girls.
someday i'll be smarter than everybody
and have a big farm in pennsylvania
and hire some immigrants
to re-enact the battle of iwo jima.
but now i play alone with my soldiers
while nobody's looking
in the privacy of my room . . .
i can kill anyone.

Image: Stephen Lewis

The Knee

Roger Aplon

The knee on the neck of George Floyd

is a knife in the heart

of those ideals

we claim

as our

sac

red

he

r

i

t

a

g

e

Back Bone

Tony Pena

Vertebrae like business
cards stacked from the base
of the brain to the top
of an executive toilet bound
tush belonging to a boss
blanched of humanity,
beholden to a buck
that only stops at the best
places, and arrogant enough
to overlook that pissing off
laborers who toil in vain will
in time make the forsaken
take up torches to burn
legal tinder to the ground.

Image: Richard Outlaw

ImaGine breathing

Timothy Brennan

ImaGine breathing
mistakEn
fOr
Resistance
and forGetting that
your badgE
conFers
constitutionaL
Obligation
for each bodY
holDing a soul
eaCh
exchAnge
demaNding
everyone's
Trust not
Be
bRoken
whEn any man
or womAn
aTtacks
not only Him
but mE
Can
the pAin
Not
spaWn
ragE
?

wisdom at fifty meters

Timothy Brennan

depth and a resemblance
two silent geometries
the anonymity
of a world in protest
a would be prophet
would take advantage
a slim endurance is breaking

the majestic sought
and laid poor
beaten down against the door
hinging in the wind
in the face in fact and theory
lives pain-
ted on black asphalt avenues
read from high above
feet scraped raw
words   color

inside it's harder to plumb
insulation cools
an emotion
inexpressible
in defense of/against selfishly

Justice

Daniel A. Villegas

Justice
We are all seeking justice
and peace
The revolution

Is here...

Sigamos adelante palante simpre pa lante

Young and old will gather to protest and lift up their voices
Strength willl come from the heavens to uplift those down on the ground
We will not run
We will not hide
We will march and dance through the many facets of life full force to
Take back what is ours
The revolution is here

Here here here here

Sigamos adelante palante simpre pa lante

Justice
We are all seeking justice
and peace
The revolution

Is here...

Sigamos adelante palante simpre pa lante

Here here here here here here here

How long have we waited for this
Streetlamps get converted into shadows
Protesters make their marks on life like if they were searching for gold
But I am searching for old
Old souls that still carry wisdom
Which at any moment can be passed down to the next generation
We are the next generation

We are the next generation
A generation
That cares and won't take no for an answer
Boarded houses leave displaced people at sea
With no one to take charge
But a memory
A memory of how it was done before
We take the streets on like if it were a fight
Laying down our arms and lifting our selves up
The revolution will not be televised
It will not be played on your television set
Instead it will be seen with people marching the streets

Streets streets streets streets.........

Sigamos adelante palante simpre pa lante

No Repeat America

Jim Eve

I am an American. One of color.
My roots cover several countries
where travesties and injustices had thrived
I was born in America and America's history
is a part of me...I am an American. America is me.

Past transgressions as part and parcel
of America's history should always be studied,
analyzed, understood and prevented
from ever happening again
by all Americans.

Removing articles of our past history is a travesty.
An erasure of the facts
a miscarriage of reality.
If we remove everything that offends someone what then?
What would America be? Hmmm...

This country built by immigrants on lands
taken from America's native people
is quilted with violence and injustices,
from its birth to what it has grown to be today.

The facts are irreversible.
The presentation of the facts at times questionable.
But what one takes away from them
is purely individual and varied.

America will always be a diverse country.
Its existence is predicated on that.
Her history will always reflect that.
Pray that it will never ever be repeated...

What We Do

Jim Eve

We protest.
We March.

We protest.
We March.

We protest.
We march
while Change on both sides of the route
shuffles its feet on the concrete sidewalks
of making a difference.

That's the way it has been for black folks in America.
Decade after Decade after Decade...

We protest.
We march
after another black soul has been taken out
by whites and placed in a grave.
Change attends the funeral as an oblivious observer.

We protest.
We march
into Deaths open arms
where we rest from marching
and no longer have to wait for change.

America's graveyards are filled with blacks,
men, women and children.
Hung, shot, burned alive while pursuing the American dream
that seems to be for whites only.

We Protest.
We march
even while Change turns its back on us.
For we believe "We Shall Overcome"...

Image: Richard Outlaw

Official Advice, In a Time of Fear

Roberta Gould

A public stance against comets is required
So put your head to the wheel
and let the flint grind
a message clear and neat
Broadcast it. Don't encrypt it
Let our enemies have it
do what they want with it
The question is complex
Keep your words simple
talk in a way
the public understands

Together, then, we will
defeat the sky
shield ourselves from death
in an original enactment
that will make us famous
So don't worry
Imagination
isn't important
We can live without it
just fine

We Are Approaching

Roberta Gould

Worried about one hundred fifty
million years ago
Timeless tomorrow
I neglect the gun in my bag
imagined service to humanity
the memory of Marlene
guilt ridden for not killing Hitler
refusing the rendez vous
he proposed

Rocks of the North
Different longitude
Then forever covered with snow
Now a new sea to be
after the melt
birds, crawlers, my kind
gone
I lament

What to do?
Worry? Curse my age?
Write this poem
that will do nothing?

I sit outside
after last night's rain
hear cheeping
from the drenched trees

Isn't the world contained
In a grain of sand?
And this moment?
The beauty of birds?
Compassion?

The earth spins
as it must
We speak
It's the nature
of our species

When is it OK?

Monet Gray

When is it OK to riot?
When can I be defiant?
Can I be noncompliant?
When can I not be silent?
I'm straight up tired
Damn... you sailed upon the motherland
And grabbed up the brother man
the black man. In fact, man we didn't do a DAMN THING
We sat back and let it happen
Never fought, never brawled never defeated the captain
That stuffed us in ships
Had us swimming in our own shit
And you want us to shut our lips? ...Bitch!
I got 2 beautiful kids
Imagine them being stripped from me, ripped from me
Taken and sold
You think that shit's funny?
It's 2020 now we Villains and you run from me
Man, I'm fed up
Don't bother to even come for me
We were raped and lynched For being black
Matter fact
We ain't retaliate — We ran away
some didn't even do that
They stayed and prayed For better days
And Can you say that day ever came?

Stop telling us to not go out and riot
Stop telling us to shut up and be quiet
Stop trying to deprive our rights
By telling us not to fight
And not to be violent
If your founders
That found us
had a right to be violent
We have a right to go out and riot!

Yo! I'mma bout to spill this tea,
Boston tea party 1773
Patriots took the tea
tossed it into the sea
They rebelled so they can rightfully be free
SO MY QUESTION: WHY YOU HERE STOPPING ME
When this country was built off of damaging others property???

Is it because you consider us property?
And it's ok if you destroy us properly?
Nah man, you tried it
Your sentiments are so biased
That's why we riot
We not fighting back quiet
We giving it all we got!
I don't even know why I asked…
Cuz we gon riot whether you like it or not!

SAY their names!

Marina Mati

SAY their names!
they came for LOVE
you HAVE no claim

FEAR begets hate
no VISION to judge
SAY their names!

you bring such PAIN
we WILL not lose
you HAVE no claim

I SEE your CHAINS
embrace the DOVE
SAY their names!

FREE of shame
they came to LIVE
you HAVE no claim

they're IN OUR HANDS
you HAVE no claim
SAY their NAMES!

independence

Marina Mati

fighting back
so glad
standing up

against hate.

they are wrong
you are strong
it's a long,

long road.

say their names
amid the flames
it's gotta change,

walk in hope.

How Many Times...

LiteSkin

Desensitized eyes are always flooded with lies
So when I size up situations,
I first look for truths that are disguised;
Are we still looking up at skies?
Is bended knees how we rise?
We've said prayers for years,
And are still in back of life's lines!
"The meek inherit the earth"
But since birth,
We've been plagued with pain
So I ask,
"What's that worth?"
How has hurt changed our positions?
It's strengthened our skins
But hasn't stopped hell from sizzling;
Our life lines are flickering,
Batteries are dying:
Yet the wicked keep bickering,
Complaining while firing...
Our people AND guns;
Affecting family funds
While taking our sons:
Broad daylight lynchings...

Back home for dinner
Without missing a drum;
Sum it all up…
The equations are still the same:
Adding stress while subtracting more lives;
Blood thirsty system's dividends
Are only different by name:
They have weakness in their veins,
Hatred masks their insecurities;
On top they remain,
And still continue their buffoonery:
There's power in words we speak:
I'm far from minor,
I don't respond to, "minority"!
I don't see supreme
And don't honor your, "supremacy"!
Since we have the tendency
To only react to fatalities,
I have a question…
How many times must we hear,
"I CAN NOT BREATHE"!?!?

Enough is Enough

Ilyanette M. Bernabel

You choose to hate, I live to elevate. Sit back and let me motivate before it's
too late. You choose to hate, you better contemplate, consequences of
your actions will leave you as bait.

This is heavy on my chest

Don't know where to begin with all this civil unrest

Innocent lives taken

Innocent lives beaten

Innocent lives locked up in cages

Innocent is the key

When will it end? When will it stop? When is enough, enough?

The same story has replayed itself over and over again

We are sick and tired of being sick and tired

You choose hate, fear and your insecurity as a way to guide your every move

You choose to hate, I live to elevate.

Elevate as a spiritual being having a human experience, elevate in consciousness

Elevate in intellect, elevate in godliness

Elevate in all things that serve me

Sit back and let me motivate before it's too late.

Melanoid brothers and sisters

There's power in unity, strength in numbers

Take the time to celebrate your brothers and sisters as you would a king or
queen

There's royalty in your bloodline, start behaving like it

There's beauty in your essence, start thriving in it

There's greatness in your presence, start walking in it

This is our time to shine, embrace it

Do more for your own, start taking care of your own and begin to build
with your own

You choose to hate, I live to elevate. Sit back and let me motivate before
it's too late. You choose to hate, you better contemplate, consequences of
your actions will leave you as bait.

Image: Eddison E Romeo, @Eyes_that_love_Art and Amir Diop @Amir.diop99

Image: Susan Slotnick

Daily Persecution

Cassandra Clarke

Our children watch and see that our dreams seem to always fall

Though we work and are even willing to crawl
That our hopes are always searched for until eternity

Though we could find a way, but we are still never guaranteed pay

It's already life, but then on top of that, we wait a lifetime for change,
       instead of living our lifetime

You then say, " I can't take this crap," the isolation, of making it
       and being Black
Your defenses are draining your emotional core, leaving you, time poor!
As your figure out the racial range of the game, but then the rules change
       and your back in pain

Loosing opportunities because of race or status even in the lower levels of fame
Choosing to "stick it out," to celebrate birthing your life, with maybe
       new opportunities to be yourself

Instead like SIDS, your birth is wiped out

Take A Stand

Penny Brodie

Drop a knee
    To celebrate your liberty
Drop a knee
    To pray for certainty.

Drop a knee
    To gather the courage
Drop a knee
    To acknowledge what the truth is.

Drop a knee
    To take a stand
Drop a knee
    To help people understand.

Drop a knee
    In strength and solidarity
Drop a knee
    To expose the disparity.

Drop a knee
    To express your rights
Drop a knee
    To continue the good fight.

Drop a knee
    To keep hope alive
Drop a knee
    For we can survive.

Drop a knee
    When you hear the angels' voices
Drop a knee
    When God asks you about your choices.

Real/Fake

Penny Brodie

Real or fake?
Patriotism is a cry to disguise
> White, male, backlash grievance.

Real or fake?
Conservatism was a place to hide but now exalts
> White, male, backlash grievance.

Real or Fake?
Liberalism is a mask for do-gooders to do good for themselves
> In the midst of, white, male, backlash grievance.

Real or fake?
Socialism is a way to absorb
> White, male, backlash grievance.

Real or fake?
Capitalism is a way to pay for
> White, male, backlash grievance.

Nativism is a label that excludes the real natives
> Who suffer the most from the white, male, backlash grievance.

Real or fake?
Trumpism is a tool to fuel
> White, male, backlash grievance.

Real or fake?

Epoch of Anger

Raphael Kosek

A little man with a big dog
    and an American flag
emblazoned on his jacket
    stopped my friend's daughter
while she was walking in Manhattan:
    "Immigrant, go back where
you belong!"
    Her daughter is tall
and olive skinned and she kept
    walking, but the flare
of the little's man's anger was
    hard like a pellet gun
and she felt the bruise on her skin,
    saw the dog's hair bristle,
smelled its clouded slobber long after
    they had passed.

Bile Eaten Flag

Tony Pena

Foamy white
venom spewed
into red and blue
Dixie cups of Kool Aid
to quench the blood
thirst of racist rabble
rousers pointing
fingers at every
perceived purveyor
of their misfortune.
Conveniently ignoring
the slander of the chief
agitator and traitor
to a country built not
by delusions of grandeur
but deeds of decency.

WELCOME

— after Ama Codjoe

Sean Foley

Into the frayed circle of my brow rings praise
to grow, the cotton leafed flower blooming violet

for the untying of strangers. My wish for you
is but milk sugar borrowed in refrain. The damp child

held to the our, of all fathers. Why is each new world
a stranger to the next? The river of shoes walks back

to blues inked into a garden. Help held, bonded
into an impatient universe, of fury and birds

pressed into ribs. Every prayer is a cage also
filled with the names of those eaten, unfeathered.

Struck, nursing dizzying wounds through distances.
All of knowledge is apology. I offer to you the pomegranate

at the heart of the lion. I crush to my chest every child
as if holding an armful of berries. Stain to me

this family of people. Root and stem, calyx and corolla.
Turn us toward the rising; open our hands to the sun.

All my life I have been told, over and under again,
'there is not enough to go around.' Yet I want

still for every emptiness to be filled. Within
this bitter and often beautiful earth, taste any flower.

Voiced, as morning sunlight, carrying breeze
unburnt. As a child I did not know what I wanted,

only that I wanted. That I was filled with wanting.
Crying out, often, to no effect. For every child

un-mothered at a border, I cry out, as a child. Learning
each uncomprehending new wail, in an empty throat.

I have not forgotten. My coppered skin flinches still.
I too was a child, waiting by a fire, holding a plate.

I hold it out again, now, to be filled. Un-torched,
so near, the harbor of welcome. Of thank you. Of please

now won't you come in, and sit. No one ever needing
to tell, anyone of us, when there was not enough.

Weeping Times

Ermira Mitre Kokomani

Troubled, time is weeping,
hung among the eyelashes,
as a prey of loss and failure.
The Earth's core is trembling.
Underground, the blood
in the roots of tortured souls,
keep boiling again, seeking justice.

In the iris of an eye,
light of hope has frozen.
We have been breathing
through masks for centuries.
Now dreary winds are blowing,
more dangerous viruses alive,
than Covid-19, bursting from
burned ashes of human love.

In between knees,
symbols of freedom inverted;
a life has just stolen another life,
choking a brother in cold blood,
by neck braking.

Hearts are squeezed like a lemon
watching George Floyd out of breathing.
Some have dried their human juice
as Saharan dessert.
Life is once more shaken,
in pain and anguish.
America has lifted the cover
of its racial pandemic!

Scarred, broken, shattered hearts in disbelief,
raging in streams, raising their voices.
Streets sheltering the memory of killings.
In turmoil, black and white, young and old,
evoking for the spirit of the dead,
until blazing the racial injustice.

A Pandemic of Love

Ermira Mitre Kokomani

Since the time of lynching,
we have been waking up
wearing the fake face of
a green dollar bill skin,
made of cotton thread
from slaves' plantations.
Living in denial of the irony
—a black life matters
less than a twenty dollar bill-
Now, the chilling death bells
are screaming globally:
"We want Justice!"

Heartbeat after heartbeat,
moment after moment,
tear after tear,
dreams and hopes
are still hanging in the air.
We are marching imperishably,
as one beacon of hope of
relentless marathoners.

Wishing the Lady of Liberty,
will wipe her tears of pain,
and smile gracefully again,
when tomorrow's dawn
will launch anti-racial sunrays,
soothing the souls' anger,
dousing the fires of hatred,
tasting the breadth of freedom.

Hence awakening our hearts,
our lost consciousness in centuries,
only to live with the ethos of spreading:
A Pandemic of Love!
A Pandemic of Harmony!
A Pandemic of Peace!
To remove all mindful remnants
of this vicious, ugly racism.

When The Saints Go Marching In

Prince A. McNally

(First published in *Jerry Jazz Musician*)

"Oh, when the saints   go marching in
  Oh when the saints   go marching in
  I want to be,   be in that number
  when the saints   go marching in"

Despite the many trials   and tribulations
of black folks,   here in the   United States of America,
as a means of survival   my people have learned
to laugh and smile   in the face of adversity.
We have learned   to mask our pain,   to weather our storms
with such a calming grace,   and quiet resilience,
more resilient than   those broken levees
that eventually gave way   to the treacherous winds,
pushing the ever-rising tide   of racism   towards the shores
of black lives,   that truly   didn't matter   to anyone.
More resilient   than the man-made storm   slamming
its treacherous winds   against   the black landscape
of Louisiana's poor.   For Hurricane Katrina
was an angry storm,   a woman scorned   who cried
crocodile tears;   it's flooding rains   suddenly came
sweeping down   upon my people like: Ethnic Cleansing.
Scores of black bodies   floating down Canal Street,   a watery grave,
a water parade,   a funeral procession.   The Fat lady sang   the blues for them
amidst the thunderous sound   of lightning ablaze with   ten thousand trumpets
ringing from the heavens   with an eerie rendition of
        "When The Saints Go Marching In"
Though the Saints never came!   The Saints never came!   FEMA never came!
FEMA never came   for the lowly ninth ward.   New Orleans, black poor.
Rescue efforts paused.   So many died,   when they didn't have to
but FEMA   never   came.   Our humanity   never   came.

Image: Susan Slotnick

~ Law of Truth ~

Kiana Queen

Speak up for those who cannot speak up for themselves;
it is our duty to make sure that justice prevails.
Look to the heavens and see that the clouds are still here,
this is sign to let us know His glorious wrath is near.
Don't be afraid because of their wicked sneers-
just rest in knowing that all hate shall be cleared.
I know it's tough to live in these days of deception,
that is why you must look within to find true direction.
Cry your tears; let them stream into the streets
because we know that the land shall go to the meek.

~ Rest In Peace... Rest In Peace... ~

Kiana Queen

{There is this heaviness that i feel.}
"I Can't Breathe... I Can't Breathe..."
(I mean like is this real?...
Someone please tell me
That this is a dream.)
Sadly, i say this is our reality.
Now Can You See?... Now Can You See...?
That because of the hate that others carry
It brings out their feeling of false superiority;
Then they take innocent lives that held promise
All for the sake of feeling like they have authority.
"I Can't Breathe... I Can't Breathe..."
"Let Me Free... Let Me Free..."
"Don't Tase Me... Don't Tase Me..."
"Lord, Help Me... Lord, Help Me..."
{There is this heaviness that i feel.}
'Rest In Peace... Rest In Peace...'
'Now You're Free... Now You're Free...'

Images: Nedwoc

Days of Hate

Gary Siegel

These are days of reckoning here in the land of the free
Yeah, land of the free that started with genocide
Land of the free that was grown upon the backs of enslaved Africans

With our long march to equality and justice
there is always the backlash, insidious and dependable
We are at a place of great change
And with a ruthless racist at the helm
   Hate roams free.

Hate runs free as we march for justice
Hate runs free as we mourn George Floyd
Hate struts around with military weapons

Now they are starting to use those guns on us
They are driving their cars, driving into us as we gather
the fever pitch is growing and everything is at stake

Don't be comfortable till everyone is comfortable

Biden Intones hollowly — This is a battle for the soul of this nation
There's a stake in the heart of this place.
And it will never be whole until
 our black people are free to walk down the street
and to flourish

Don't get too comfortable
please don't get too comfortable
don't you get comfortable
till everyone is free.

Rage

Don Badgley

tentacles of rage embrace us
blisters weeping in its grip
rage, our overseer and his whip
venomous rage, defiling our skin
rage, our helpless limbic rejoinder
to filthy injustice
rage, crushing out our breath
vomiting from our shredded lips
in righteous gasps
RAGE, our oppressor's final victory

At The Rally

Daniel Brown

Playing
On summer grass
A small brown child tries
To stack round plastic candles;
They fall.

Once more
She tries, turning
Them over; will that work?
Or next to each other in tidy
Short rows.

She learns
With small fingers
On summer grass, intent
Like old mister story book moon
Rising.

She learns
Stacking candles
With small brown fingers what
All children must always be free
To learn.

While deep
Beneath her hands
A hot desert removed
Caged dark cousins cry out for
Madre.

As uniformed goblins with twisted claws
And blood moon nightmare eyes
Force them to suckle
From breasts of leaking sand.

No More Gone —for Odetta

Daniel Brown

The old song: "Another Man Done Gone."
"I didn't know his name" We never did know!
 Chain gang done gone
Levee Camp done gone
Sharecropper done gone
Brutally done gone, expendable done gone
    The attitude was:
        (As Memphis Slim said quoting white boss men
        "If you kill a mule, I'll buy another one
          If you kill a nigger, I'll hire another one".)

Women done gone just as much, just as anonymous.
Worked to death gone under piles of rich white laundry gone
Raped gone
All alone gone with all these kids gone because they
Destroyed the family unit gone with Chain gangs and Levee Camps
Gone! Always done, gone, gone!

But Now: "Another Man Done Gone"
We do know his name.
We saw and heard his dying pain
The whole world's demanding change.

And the strength of a people is hardly gone. Never gone.
Folks fought back against being slaves, rain away in droves
Never gone
Folks who demanded the right to vote (and still do)
Never gone
Folks who bared the brunt of the fire hose, to eat
At a goddamn Woolworth lunch counter!! Never gone!
Never more gone! Done!!

White Is Not Always Right

Mary Louise Kiernan

Is your complacency startled?

You ask for the raw truth.
The husband had their children chant:
White Is Right!
White Is Right!
White Is Right!
He then sneered, "Bleeding heart liberal."
My once lifelong friend rolled her eyes,
"Oh, that's just Joe being Joe. A drink?"
How long could I stay unconscious?

Hush Mout'

Brianna Knight

Some people's grandmommas ain't say nothin
They'll tell you that's how they survived
How they kept they kin
Kept the cloth woven together

Some people's mommas ain't say nothing That's how they ate
Kept the lights on, The stove hot, The bed cold
"She ain't nothing special, he ain't no good."

Some people's sistas ain't say nothin
They ain't pick you up, Heal your wounds
Ain't warn you bout the barbed wire
The burning sensation while realizing you too will deal with God

There were folks that ain't have a choice
No breath left in their body
Couldn't make it past the sea
But you did, you're here
So what you gon' do about it?

For My Kings

Brianna Knight

The Devil is very black and white
Yet paints in grey
for a man to find loopholes
Chain himself to the cabin
Forever wailing to the moon
As retribution for being born
And in the same breath
Punish a black woman for breathing

So paranoid about the white man
He renounces his violence
Blaming it on scripture
And beats his love into an early grave
Claims it reincarnation

I hear we were once Kings and Queens
remember the queen still took her lashes
In silence while standing on a pulpit
She still belonged to the Kingdom

Black women speak in a lifetime of blues
Bit by the babies we once delivered
Being somebody's mother isn't enough
For our mothers took those lashes without a crown
And ate those punches to have a pot to piss in
And weeped in their own laps

It is oh so lonely to be in love with death
It is oh so painful to lick the wounds

Wrap To Get Her

Sarah Vogwill June

The darkest of places I trust. The brightest know nothing.
A shiny strut, the pleased cajole. Purity
exposes itself, with out wondering.

Yes these dark places, they secret themselves to know
one, lingering rearview drops of reflection,
gathered for density, sift for night, encrypted for power.

Precious, solidified by repeated poundings,
the mind wanders. Seeking light for what glory & sunshine
is very implicated. Gathered by hands, by hearts

By affliction stock, shore & simulate.
Slippery at dusk, forgetful at dawn,
in its grasp, invisible to you my friend, in its gaze.

So much to be remembered
as you stare at your breakfast cup. What is there in the depths,
what is almost not there?

Take a drink, black coffee on your lip,
black thoughts on your tongue
tied, hamstrung, face down, kissing
the pavement just this once, last time.

I Know Not

Sharon Ferrante

the color of fear,
how does a philosopher find it?
is it on a page?

Is it in a year? Like 1974
when I fell in love for the first time
laying on his couch with no friends, only him.

I rub my eyes, because I don't understand!
No poets crown can show me,
I've tried.

Bewilderment in my rusted tears,
all these years,

I Know Not the color of fear.

Normalized

Dana Hunter

There will be found a standing ground.
A statement made without word.
A cry for ears to hear its plea
The final balance to be found.

We are not invisible
the forgotten to be hidden.
Obscure names with memories charred.
We share one race to which we all belong.
Illness doesn't cancel your membership card.

Our minds and our lives are not cursed.
Once we are mentioned you disperse.

If you can't touch it or cure it
It's pushed to the side.
No longer. No longer.
Our voices will rise.

The time has come you've heard the rest.
We are first in line, and it is YOU we will test.
A final point of discourse must take place.

I am not subhuman.

We all belong to the same race.

For Harriet

Greg Correll

If you cry
and I close my eyes to you
I am not free. If you stumble
and I don't catch you, help you stand,
I am not free. If you are sick
and spill upon the floor and I
complain about the mess?
I am not free. If you are in bondage
and I do not fill my fists with sledges and saws—
unbraid the whip, unload the pistol, risk all?
I am not free. If you are ground up,
used by evil men, left to bleed, alone,
and I change the channel?
I am not free. If you are almost gone,
reach from the winding sheet,
terror like pepper under the skin,
not ready to go—and need my word, my hand?
and I just, you know, can't deal with that,
hope you understand, just can't?
I am not free. If you offer a rock
and I call it sand, if you suffer fire
and I call it friction, if you ask for lovingkindness
and I call it in, call for the check, call it a day?
If you live beside me—and you do—
but are not free?
I am not free.

Image: Greg Correll

Yodel 16 (riot & dream)

Mike Jurkovic

Here where the odds go down
as the sun comes up we riot and dream
and riot again. Moved by more,
we dream drearily of Heaven
Bearing nostalgia for discarded things.

But I tend not to care how history judges,
Brings our misfirings up to the fore.
I tend to think of now as prologue and
How I make our story better from here.

Image: Mike Jurkovic

SAY THE NAMES

Breonna Taylor, Nina Pop, Medgar Evers, Trayvon Martin, George Floyd, Pamela Turner, AJ Sutton, Robert Fuller, Dominique Fells, Sean Reed, Tony Mcdade, Sandra Bland, Zoe Spears, Danye Jones, Philando Castile, Kirvan Fortuin, Ahmaud Arbery, Cameron Green, Christopher Kapessa, Sam DuBose, David McAtee, Pearlie Golden, Eric Garner, Rekia Boyd, Freddie Carlos Gray Jr, Wyatt Outlaw, Michael Noel, Eugene Williams, Darren Seals, Rayshard Brooks, Emmet Till, Addie Mae Collins, Cynthia Wesley, Carol Denise McNair, Laura & L, D, Nelson, Oscar Grant, Eric Harris, Jesse Washington, James Scurlock, Stephon Clark, Nathaniel Pickett Jr, Sean Bell, Carole Robertson, Riah Milton, Brooklyn Lindsey, Atatiana Jefferson, Botham Jean, Isaiah Lewis, Shereese Francis, Chanel Scurlock, Paris Cameron, Ágatha Félix, Elijah Glay, Renisha McBride, Modesto Reyes, Deandre Joshua, Kevin Higgenbotham, Jazzaline Ware, Patrick Dorismond, Steve Taylor, Jamar Clark, Ashanti Carmon, William Green, Muhlaysia Booker, Maurice Gordon, Bettie Jones, Dana Martin, Adrian Medearis, Roy Nelson, Mark Duggan, Claire Legato, Dante Parker, Phillip White, Shantee Tucker, Michael Dean, Leroy Browning, Miguel Espinal, Tiara Thomas, Tyrone West, Chad Gordon, Obe Cox, Regis Korchinski-Paquet, George Armwood, Alonzo Smith, Dominic Hutchinson, Ahmed Erekat, Elijah McClains, Meagan Marie Hockaday, Emantic Fitzgerald Bradford Jr, Tatyana Hargrove, Jordan Edwards, Hadiya Pendleton, Aiyana Mo'Nay Stanley Jones, Ryan L, Stokes, Lamontez Jones, Rayshaun Cole, Paterson Brown, Michael Brown, Jamel Floyd, Douglas Lewis, Thomas Moss, Calvin McDowell, Eliza Woods, Thomas Shipp, Abram Smith,

Shukri Abdi, Junior Prosper, Wayne Wheeler, Lavante Biggs, Belly Mujinga, James Carney III, Asshams Manley, Christian Taylor, Felix Kumi, Timothy Russell, Malissa Williams, Jeremy McDole, Albert Joseph Davis, Anthony Ashford, Tamir E, Rice, Korryn Gaines, Darrius Stewart, Akai Gurley, Yvette Smith, George Mann, Sasha Wall, LaVena Johnson, Sarah Reed, Adama Traoré, Edson Da Costa, Rashan Charles, Nunu Cardoso, Latasha Harlins, Tawana McGowan, Richard Perkins Jr, Laquan McDonald, Salvado Ellswood, Jonathan Sanders, Charlemagne Péralte, Kendrick Johnson, Yahira Nesby, Spencer Lee McCain, Kevin Bajoie, Zamiel Crawford, Kris Jackson, Edward Crawford, Sherrie Walker, Michelle 'Tamika' Washington, Richard Gregory Davis, Markus Clark, Jule Dexter, Lorenzo Hayes, Dennis Plowden Jr, Eric Reason, Herbert Lee, James Earl Chaney, Stephen Biko, Jamee Johnson, William Brooks, Ells Persons, Sean Rigg, Jessica Williams, D'Angelo Stallworth, Dajuan Graham, Brandon Glenn, Kiki Fantroy, Dominick Wise, Trevor Smith, Lawrence Hawkins, David Felix, Terry Lee Chatman, William Chapman, Samuel Harrell, Juan May, Kenneka Jenkins, Kendra James, Norman Cooper, Walter Scott, Tarika Wilson, Donald Ivy, Shelly Frey, Amadou Diallo, Malik Williams, Samuel DuBose, Dominick Ray Wise, Tracey Single, Jason Moland, Bobby Gross, Brandon Jones, Isadore Banks, Askari Roberts, Terrance Moxley, Anthony Hill, Tyisha Miller, Keith Childress, Tony Robinson, Alan de Souza Lima. Damariontae Brown, Darrell Gatewood, Deontre Dorsey, Thomas Allen Jr, Lavall Hall, Frank Smart, Emerald Black, Calvon Reid, Gerdle Moise, Terry Price, Natasha McKenna, Jeremy Lett, Alvin Haynes, Ronell Foster, Jonathan Ferrell, Marielle Franco, João Pedro Mattos, Artago Damon Howard, Ervin Leon Edwards, Antwon Rose Jr, Gregory Hill Jr, Matthew Ajibade, Denali Berries Stuckey, Terence Crutcher, Alton Sterling, Alfred Olango, Michael Lee Marshall, Olaseni Lewis, John H, Crawford III, Tommy Yancy, Ariane McCree, Ricky Deangelo Hinkle, Monika Diamond, Ramarley Graham, Jamarion Robinson, Tomell Hurd, Shantel Davis, Alejandro Vargas Martinez, Ja'Quarius Taylor, Tanisha Anderson, Jerame C, Reid, Miriam Carey, Jason Harrison, Bennie Branch, Tyre King, Lemuel Penn, Joe Huff, India M, Beaty, Mario Clark, Ernest Satterwhite, Lavon King, Iretha Lilly, Veronica Woodward, Jayvis Benjamin, Virgil Lamar Ware, Andre Horton, Cynthia Fields, Kevin Matthews, Kendra Diggs, Kaldrick Donald, Deborah Danner, Henry Dumas, Magruder

Fletcher, George Junius Stinney Jr, Frazier B, Baker & Julia Baker, Henry Smith, Joe Pullen, Darrien Hunt, Elbert Williams, Eugene William, Robert E, Robinson, Lemuel Walters, Frank Livingston, Dave Tillis, Mrs, Wise, Anthony Crawford, Sam Hose, Lamar "Ditney" Smith, Cordella Stevenson, Slab Pitts, Malcom Harsch, Jule Perry, James Howard Willie, Michael Donald, Mary Turner, Martin Luther King Jr, Malcolm X, Fred Hampton

These are just some of the lives lost at the hands of hatred and injustice.
Rest Easy to the millions of others whose names we know and haven't known…
(and even so, their precious lives will never be forgotten…)
List assembled by Kiana Queen

THE POETS

Poet Gold, Editor —A rare talent who grabs you by the heart and says "Recognize" —
Poet, author, performer, songwriter, community "Artivist" and speaker, Bettina "Poet
Gold" Wilkerson is pushing the boundaries of poetry and the spoken word. Living
with a chronic illness since childhood, Poet Gold, or as she is affectionately known,
"Gold", brings a soul-searching insight about the human existence, love, dreams, chal-
lenges, and triumph.

Appointed the 2017 and 2018 NYS Dutchess County Poet Laureate, Poet
Gold is the recipient of numerous awards. With countless recitations, she has opened
for Grammy-nominated artists and has spoken at renowned organizations such as
Omega Institute and Self Employment in the Arts.

Presently she is the co-host for the iHeart Radio podcast "Finding Out with
Pete and The Poet Gold". Her distinct voice will be heard, playing the role of God, in
the upcoming animated short film "The Creation" poem by James Weldon Johnson,
directed by award winning animated film maker, Steve Leeper.

Poet Gold is an activist of the heart. Her words inspire to explore the essence
of humanity. To learn more about "Poet Gold" visit one of her pages in social media:
facebook.com/Poet-Gold-BGW-408311444664/
linkedin.com/in/poetgoldbgw
iheart.com/podcast/481-peter-and-the-poet-gold-30383287/
instagram.com/_poetgold_/

Roger Aplon, has published thirteen books: Most recently: *Mustering What's Left –
Selected & New Poems – 1976 – 2017* from Unsolicited Press. He lives in Beacon, N Y
& publishes the poetry magazine: *Waymark – Voices of the Valley*. You can read and hear
examples of his work at: rogeraplon.com

Don Badgley is a Quaker from Gardiner, NY. and by profession is an insurance coun-
selor. He is married to Tracy L. Badgley, CPA and has two grown daughters, Marissa
and Alanna.

Ilyanette M. Bernabel, a self-proclaimed DominiRican (Dominican and Puerto Rican)
born in Bronx, New York and raised in Poughkeepsie, New York, is an actress, poet,
theatre artist, and Curatorial Assistant at Longue Vue House and Gardens based in the
New Orleans metropolitan area. Her acting credits include Young Tough in *Mother
Courage and Her Children* (Southern Rep Theatre), Johnna in *August: Osage Coun-
ty* (Southern Rep Theatre), and various roles at the State University of New York,
Purchase College. She holds a BA in Theatre and Performance Studies from SUNY,
Purchase College, and a MA in Museum Studies from Southern University at New
Orleans.

Tim Brennan is a poet, painter and woodworker who has lived and worked in Prov-
idence, San Francisco, Brooklyn, and now New Paltz, NY, where he has been reno-
vating his old house for over thirty years. His poems have been published in *La Presa,
Awosting Alchemy, The Blue Collar Review*, and *The Chronogram*, and in the 2011 and the
2014 edition of the *Wallkill Valley Writers' Anthology* and the *2020 Anthology of Calling
All Poets*. With Susan Chute he co-curates the reading series, Next Year's Words in
New Paltz, NY.

Penny Wickham Brodie is a licensed speech language pathologist. She hosts *Mingus
Moments* on WVKR 91.3FM. The inaugural Poet Laureate of Sullivan County, NY.

Daniel Brown is a retired Special Education teacher. He has been interested in poetry
for much of his life but only began writing a decade ago. His poems cover a variety of
subjects from Japanese short forms to poems about music and social issues. Daniel reads
regularly at CAPS (Calling All Poets) in New Paltz N.Y. He resides in Red Hook, N.Y.

Cassandra Clarke is a Master Level Social Worker having earned a BA degree at SUNY New Paltz and a MSW at Fordham University Graduate School. I like to poeticize about all aspects of life. I have had the opportunity to bring several poetry experiences to life through video. (Nilevideo) As life rolls on I am also looking forward to creating a book of poems and doing a future Podcast.

Chris Collins—Chris Collins considers himself a minor poet with a brief portfolio and high hopes. He earned a master's degree from Columbia University, then pursued doctoral studies at SUNY Albany. Chris taught psychology at Marist College in Poughkeepsie and at SUNY Ulster, both in NY. A five-year exploration of nature photography was followed by a stint in local politics, then the creation of a 501C(3) comedy festival that ran for five years, its profits donated to survivors of domestic violence and human trafficking. Chris's poems have been published in several Hudson Valley and national outlets. krisco1@hvc.rr.com

Greg Correll was a Fellow at the CUNY Writers Institute in 2017, where he worked closely with Leo Carey *(The New Yorker)* and Jonathan Galassi *(FSG)*. Wrote about his Parkinson's diagnosis *(Salon)*, and sexual assaults in jail at 14 *(Medium)*. Works found in a half-dozen essay/poetry anthologies, including *Into Sanity* (2019), co-edited by Mark Vonnegut. Two short plays produced, one off-Broadway. A freelance editor, he loves helping writers improve and polish. Three ferocious, brilliant daughters. gcorrell@smallpackages.com

Amir Diop is an Indigenous African American male born and raised in Brooklyn, New York. Amir is a young emerging street artist taking his abilities to the soho. He uses his style to express how he views the world going around him. Amir is an award winning artist from conception arts. Amir has also had articles written by verge and esquire magazine. He has had his work appear on channel 1 nyc news. Amir is 21 years young and he is working to make a difference to the world. He is fighting for justice against the injustice in America.

Jim Eve is the originator of the Calling All Poets Inc. Calling All Poets was a program that originated at the Howland Cultural Center when Jim was a board member there back in 1999. Along the way he partnered with Mike Jurkovic and together with the help of long time supporters move the program forward. The program obtained its own non-profit status in June of 2014 and currently resides at the Roost Gallery and Studio in New Paltz, NY. Jim, who writes poetry whenever the mood strikes him, considers himself more of a facilitator of poetry than a poet.

Sharon Ferrante: "When I discovered CAPS, my love of poetry was rekindled. With their dedication to welcoming you, I feel a belonging. Like a brushstroke from the colorful palette of the spoken word. Showing kindness of diversity, a collage of Hudson Valley Awe. As they give of their time, an encouraged poet hears a little song. Thank you CAPS, a jaw-dropper, recommended to all!"

Sean Foley: "I am the son of an immigrant mother. My father was the son of an immigrant mother. My father's father was the son of immigrant parents. I can remember a time, from when I was in grammar school, before Dr. King was assassinated, there was a tradition of giving the gift of an African Violet, to a new neighbor, as a sign of welcome. We live in troubling times, equal to any our nation has ever known."

Roberta Gould—"I began writing in my 20's; by age 30, full commitment to poetry, though not sure where I wanted to go. To say or Not to say? Early work had surreal & dream influence...attempting accessibility. Cadence of language and musicality important. I try to make each day worthy for the air I breath, and do not force myself to write. Poems published widely in mags and anthologies. *Woven Lightning*, Spuyten Duyvil Press and *Talk When You Can*, Presa Press, books 12 and 13, published in 2019. More info, credits and poems at web site: robertagould.net."

Monet Gray aka TestiMonet is a full time educator and mother. She's also the owner of a media company called TestiMonet Productions LLC. She has written multiple short films, feature films, plays and poems. Monet has had a love for poetry and began writing her first few poems at age 15. She taught poetry workshops to adults and children and hopes to continue to teach this craft to other hungry individuals that love the art of spoken word. She's just completed her first poetry book (and web series), "Lyrical Biblical Tales."

Dana I. Hunter published her first short story *'Pieces of Gray'* in Adelaide Literary Magazine. Her Screenplay *'STEVI'* won Honorable Mention in the first 'Scriptapalooza' contest. She received her B.A. in Communications from Upsala College and continued her studies at Emerson College in Boston.

Kate Hymes, poet, workshop leader and writing consultant, lives in New Paltz, New York. She has nurtured writers in the Hudson Valley through her leadership of Wallkill Valley Writers. Kate's recent publication is a chapbook, True Grain. Published in three regional anthologies edited by Codhill Press: *Riverine: An Anthology of Hudson Valley Writers, Slant of Light: Contemporary Women Writers of the Hudson Valley,* and *Reflecting Pool: Poets and the Creative Process*—and *Gathering Ground: Cave Canem 10 Year Anniversary Anthology,* University of Michigan Press. Kate edited *wVw Anthologies 2011* and *2015,* containing memoir, short fiction and poetry.

Mike Jurkovic is President, Calling All Poets. 2016 Pushcart nominee. Full length titles: *Blue Fan Whirring, smitten by harpies,* & *shiny banjo catfish.* Chapbook: *Eve's Venom.* Anthologies: *Reflecting Pool: Poets & the Creative Process, WaterWrites: A Hudson River Anthology,* and *Riverine: Anthology of Hudson Valley Writers* (Codhill Press, 2018, 2009, 2007) Features and CD reviews appear in *All About Jazz, Van Wyck Gazette, Maverick Chronicles.* He is the Tuesday night host of Jazz Sanctuary, WOOC 105.3 FM, Troy, NY. He loves Emily most of all. mikejurkovic.com

Mary Louise Kiernan's poetry has been published in The New York Times and elsewhere. She was awarded the 2015 Poetry Prize co-sponsored by Tempe Public Library and Arizona State University. Her full-length collection, *The Gift of Glossophobia,* is forthcoming from Kelsay Books.

Brianna Knight: I'm a 22 year old African American poet from Spring Valley, New York. I am a member of the Urban Lyrics poetry collective, established at SUNY New Paltz in 2007. I've been writing poetry for the last four years, publishing my work in zines as well as working on a personal poetry book titled Ladybug. My poetry stems from experiences I've faced crossing sexism, racism and other traumas. I write free verse and sometimes haikus. I hope through my words, I'm able to spread healing and explain history's cycles.

Ermira Mitre Kokomani is a published poet in a few countries around the world and an avid member of Montclair Write Group in Montclair New Jersey, and reads her poetry regularly in Open Mic events.

Raphael Kosek's poems have appeared in such venues as *Poetry East, Catamaran,* and *Briar Cliff Review.* Her latest chapbook, *Rough Grace,* won the 2014 Concrete Wolf Chapbook Prize. Her new book, *American Mythology,* was released in 2019. She has been a supporter of CAPS since their genesis and feels they have contributed to both her own growth as a poet and the very rich poetry culture blooming in the Hudson Valley. She teaches English at Marist College and Dutchess Community College in the Hudson Valley where her students keep her real. She is the 2019 Dutchess County Poet Laureate.

Stephanie Laterza is the author of poetry chapbook, *The Psyche Trials* (Finishing Line Press, 2019) and a SU-CASA 2018 award recipient from the Brooklyn Arts Council. Stephanie's work has appeared in *L'Éphémère Review, First Literary Review-East, Ovunque Siamo, A Gathering of the Tribes, Newtown Literary, Literary Mama, San Francisco Peace & Hope, The Nottingham Review, Akashic Books, Obra/Artifact, Pratik, Latina Outsiders: Remaking Latina Identity* (Routledge, 2019), *Raising Mothers,* and the *Brownstone Poets 2020 Anthology.* Stephanie's poem, "Homecoming," is forthcoming in the Lamorinda Arts Council's video highlighting the anthology, San Francisco Peace and Hope: Light the Sky. Follow Stephanie: Instagram: @stef3rd.

Stephen Lewis is a painter and printmaker who is work is primarily concerned with art of observation of both the sociopolitical and natural world. In that sense, his work is unique in that it inhabits two distinct genres; naturalism and political art, but the artist sees his practice as incorporating the same principals in the creation of both bodies of work—they are tied together by the artists unique ability to articulate realities that only become obvious thru monastic observation and study. His work has been reviewed or featured in diverse publications including; *The Washington Post, Art News, Timeout, High Times, Casa Vogue,* and *The New Yorker.*

Born and raised in New York City's Lower East Side, **LiteSkin** (Living It Through Every Situation Known In Nature) is a HipHop/SpokenWord artist who exudes passion and grit in everything he spits. Since young, he's been focused on empowering all who listen with his ability to bend words and use multi-leveled meanings with his wordplay. Appropriately titled the "WordSmith With A Purpose," he has spread his messages for many years. Lite has performed in and hosted countless events and left his mark on all microphones. His music and talents can be found on all musical streaming sites and YouTube.

Lucy, artist: "Arrest the cops that killed Breonna Taylor."
Instagram: @aesopslucy; site: aesopslucy.com; aesopslucy@gmail.com

Matt Maley is a working artist with thirty years in the fields of Illustration, Sculpture and Design. His illustrations have appeared in publications such as Marvel, Disney and Children's Television Workshop. His sculptures and published work sell around the world. Matt is also Associate Creative Director for Marist College in Poughkeepsie. Matt lives in New Paltz with his family and friends. mattmaley.com

Marina Mati has featured in NYC and the Hudson Valley at performance venues, cafes, bars, and bookstores. Her poetry has also been featured by Jonathan Wolfman on his Passionate Justice podcast. Publishing credits include many anthologies, *Napalm Health Spa / MAP*, editor Jim Cohn, and BigCityLit, editor Nick Johnson, among others. Her chapbook is entitled cave-speak. Calling All Poets has been her poet-home for over 15 years and she has served on the board. Marina is from NYC and now lives in the Hudson Valley. I am pleased to be taking a stand with my fellow-poets.

Prince A. McNally is a Brooklyn-born poet, writer, essayist, philosopher and activist whose work (though quite eclectic) focuses primarily on the human condition, and social justice. His poems have appeared in Dissident Voice, Jerry Jazz -Musician, TUCK Magazine, Leaves of Ink, The Blue Mountain Review, and First Literary East just to name a few, as well as several anthologies. He is currently working on his first collection of poetry due out in early 2021.

Nedwoc loves every trudging soul. Most days.

Jean O'Neill has been on this earth almost 60 years. Daily goals are to do the right thing and make someone laugh, nailing one of these is considered a pretty good day. Jean is a writer but does other things to put $ in the bank. She counts her blessings daily: roof, food, healthy children & family, great neighbors, hairy dogs, phone poles and a room with an awesome view.

Richard Outlaw: "In describing my work, many have said that my landscape pictures are vibrant in color and serene in nature. My impressionistic paintings focus on the oppression, struggle, politics, and richness of African Americans. I present these aspects of our life in America in abstract paintings as well. My objective is to capture the strength, weakness, pain and glory of my people as they were in the past and as they are now." Richard Outlaw is a graduate of Adelphi University.

Tony Pena was the 2017-2018 Poet Laureate for the city of Beacon, New York. Recently some of his poetry and fiction have found homes in *1870, As it Ought to Be, Horror, Sleaze & Trash, Misfit Magazine, Museum of Poetry, Poetry Breakfast, Red Fez, The Dope Fiend Daily, The Rye Whiskey Review,* and other journals. A volume of poetry and flash fiction, *Blood and Beats and Rock n Roll,* is available at Amazon. A chapbook of poetry, *Opening night in Gehenna,* is available from author. Colorful compositions and caterwauling with a couple of chords can be seen at: youtube.com/tonypenapoetry, and facebook.com/tonypenapoetry

Kiana Queen is an artist who fights for humanity. With her soul-searching words she seeks to help everyone not only find a reason to love themselves but to also love others. She is best known for her literary works that evoke emotions that causes one to gain a new perspective on life. Kiana Queen is the future; she is also the now...

Cheryl A. Rice's poems have appeared in *Home Planet News, Rye Whiskey Review, Up The River,* and *Misfit Magazine,* among others. Recent chapbooks include *Until the Words Came* (Post Traumatic Press), co-authored with Guy Reed, and *Love's Compass* (Kung Fu Treachery Press). Rice lives in New York's Hudson Valley. Her blog is at: http://flyingmonkeyprods.blogspot.com/.

Douglass Ridgeway has been writing poetry since his teen years. Recently, he has been known to have public poetic conversations through posting of poetry on phone poles in his neighborhood. These poems were created as a call and response between two poets after a conversation about social justice one evening. Douglass is also a web developer, graphic designer, and the owner of RAW Design Lab, a web design firm (www. RAWdesignlab.com).

Eddison E. Romeo was born in Trinidad and Tobago on July 22 nd 1977 and grew up in the South Bronx. He currently resides in Newburgh New York. Eddison's work portrays the ideology that color opens up one's third eye, which is one's soul. Seeing the colors in the different ways it can be seen, is different from other Artist for Eddison because he is color blind. He ,sole heartedly relies on his imagination, emotions and feelings but more importantly deep down inside , which will take his paintings to a whole other level. He has completed over Sixty-paintings where by using various mediums and colors, his work comes to life. By using explosive, robust and invigorating colors, you will be able to see his work come to life. His vision is to have such an effect on the human eye/soul that it takes the viewer to a whole new level of imagination and creativity.

Amanda Russell is a stay-at-home mom who lives with her husband, two children and a dog in New York's Hudson Valley. She published a poetry chapbook, *Barren Years*, with Finishing Line Press in 2019. She recently won Editor's Choice Award in the 2020 Annual Poetry Contest run by SpiritFirst.org. Her poems have appeared in *The Lincoln Underground* and more recently in *Social Unity*, a CelebrateWomxn845 zine that raises money for organizations dedicated to feeding families across the Hudson Valley during the COVID-19 pandemic. You can find links to her published poems, interviews, articles, media accounts and recent readings at poetrussell.wordpress.com.

Stephanie JT Russell is the author of poetry chapbook, *The Psyche Trials* (Finishing Line Press, 2019) and a SU-CASA 2018 award recipient from the Brooklyn Arts Council. Stephanie's work has appeared in *L'Éphémère Review, First Literary Review-East, Ovunque Siamo, A Gathering of the Tribes, Newtown Literary, Literary Mama, San Francisco Peace & Hope, The Nottingham Review, Akashic Books, Obra/Artifact, Pratik, Latina Outsiders: Remaking Latina Identity* (Routledge, 2019), *Raising Mothers,* and the *Brownstone Poets 2020 Anthology*. Stephanie's poem, "Homecoming," is forthcoming in the Lamorinda Arts Council's video highlighting the anthology, *San Francisco Peace and Hope: Light the Sky.* Follow Stephanie: Instagram: @stef3rd.

Gary Siegel: "I am a Poet. My writing is driven by journeys into nature as well as the inner journeys. When I found the CAPS, I found an environment. I would say that at CAPs – we take our poetry seriously, but not necessarily ourselves. There is the feeling that the readers here are deeply dug into their craft, while all are welcome and encouraged to work their art. The place has that feel. After a night at the Roost I want to love reading more and I want to get better. I also want very much to come back."

Susan Slotnick has brought the joy of modern dance to incarcerated men for the past 20 years. Her choreography deals with serious themes to inspire audiences and students toward social justice activism. Since 1988, Susan's been a featured columnist for The New Paltz Times. For ten years her painting *Compassionate Baby* was displayed in the Sloan-Kettering Hospital's Pediatric Oncology Waiting Room. In 2010 Susan was the Huffington Post's "Greatest Woman of The Day." A documentary profile about her, *The Game Changer,* won first prize at both the Cannes Film Festival and The Harlem Film Festival.

Meghan Sullivan is an educator and poet living in New Orleans. A NY native, she has represented SUNY New Paltz as a two time competitor at the College Unions Poetry Slam invitational. Meghan is also an alumna of Urban Lyrics, a rap, spoken word, and poetry collective born out of the Hudson Valley in Upstate New York. Meghan holds a Bachelors of Arts Degree in Sociology and Women's Gender and Sexuality Studies and looks forward to pursuing a MFA in poetry. Her current works are a curious exploration of what it means to be a transplant living in New Orleans.

Daniel A. Villegas is a bilingual spoken word poetry from Colombia and Warwick NY. He has been performing for over 15 years all around the country. His unique blend of Spanish and English in his poetry separate him from most styles heard. He speaks from his heart. With topics such as social change, love, life and living free he delivers a message with hope and meaning. To see Daniel perform is to experience humility and love for what music has to offer in today's day and age.

Sarah Vogwill lives in Brooklyn & West Saugerties. After decades focused on visual art, she now takes refuge in writing and turns her attention to local sustainability initiatives & movement building with *Extinction Rebellion NYC*.

Bruce Weber is the author of six books of poetry, the most recent of which is *There are Too Many Words in My House* (Rogue Scholars Press, 2019). He is also a historian of American Art, and writes and produces the blog learningwoodstockartcolony.com.

Regi Wroteit is an eclectic writer and spoken word poet who never leaves home without a notebook and pen. Originally from the Capital District, Regi moved to the Hudson Valley after graduating from New Paltz College. She has performed spoken word poetry at local open mics and arts festivals, such as the O+ Festival and First Fridays in Poughkeepsie. Currently, Regi is working on her first novel, which tells the story of a young woman overcoming workplace bullying. In her spare time, Regi enjoys learning the Spanish language and getting advice from the book of Proverbs.
Writing is like breathing.

Sandra Yannone published her debut collection *Boats for Women with Salmon Poetry* in 2019. Salmon will publish *The Glass Studio* in 2022. Her poems and book reviews have appeared in numerous print and online journals including *Ploughshares, Poetry Ireland Review, Boyne Berries, Sweet, Live Encounters, Women's Review of Books,* and *Lambda Literary Review.* She also has written a series of essays on the intersections between poetry and social justice for *Works in Progress.* She currently hosts *Cultivating Voices LIVE Poetry Open Mic* on Facebook on Sundays. Visit her at www.sandrayannone.com.

PAIR POETRY: **Jean O'Neill** and **Douglass Ridgeway**
"These poems were created as a call and response between two neighbors after a conversation about social justice one evening.

IMAGE (DETAIL) CREDITS, BACK COVER

Top row, from left: Richard Outlaw, Nedwoc (for Kate Hymes), Stephen Lewis

2nd Row: Greg Correll, Matt Maley

3rd Row: Susan Slotnick, Lucy